THE SMART BOOK OF RECIPES AND TIPS

ANN LOUISE HOOD

Happy Cooking Karen

The Smart School of Cookery

Essex

the smart
school of cookery

2 3 4 5 6 7 8 9 10

PRINTED IN CHINA

Visit our website at www.thesmartschoolofcookery.com

Designed by Andrew Pepper

ISBN: 978-1-78280-130-6

Contents

NOT JUST A COOKBOOK

This is not just a cookbook, it's also full of the tips and techniques you need to make the perfect dish to restaurant standard in little time and with little effort.

I started my cookery school in 2007 as a hobby. Now the Smart School of Cookery has become my full time career and within 6 years has grown to 6 cookery schools. All the chefs at the schools are either celebrity chefs or trained by myself, using all my menus and recipes.

My previous career had been in teaching music for over 30 years and entering over 3000 students of all ages into exams, with an average pass rate of 98%.

When my daughter came along, I also started an interior design business alongside my father's property renovation business.

From an early age, I'd travelled with my parents and been introduced to some fabulous culinary experiences, but the bug really caught hold after my daughter and a friend entered me (without my knowledge) for the BBC television programme Masterchef. I mixed my love of cooking with the artistic and teaching background to make my hobby the best job I have ever had.

My philosophy is that food is all about taste and texture. You should be able to taste every ingredient you have used.

TIPS

PARCHMENT

I mainly use parchment instead of foil; it doesn't stick.

STIRRING

Don't keep stirring as stirring slows down the cooking process by dropping the temperature of the pan/food.

KNIFE SKILLS

I highly recommend a knife skills lesson; it only takes a couple of hours. This will speed up preparation and you will enjoy it so much more and of course it improves your knife safety. You will learn the art of filleting, boning and professional vegetable cuts which are great skills to have. Using the right knives; you only need 2 good ones; a chef's knife and a paring knife.

Never put sharp knives in the dishwasher as it blunts them. Sharpen knives every time you use them with a diamond steel. A round steel only keeps the 'V' shape, it's the diamond steel that actually sharpens.

MARINATING

Never marinade overnight. Long marination was used years ago to disguise meat or fish that was 'past its best' or of poor quality. Marinade for no more than an hour so you can taste both the meat/fish and the marinade ingredients. However, if you are using any citrus, alcohol, soy sauce or vinegar (or anything else acidic) then marinade for a *maximum of 3 minutes*; these ingredients will start 'curing', which is a form of cooking and will turn your meat or fish hard.

INGREDIENTS

Always taste your dishes before you serve. Remember, you can always add ingredients; you can't take them out.

All the ingredients will be a different age, strength and quality so always add slowly, slowly until its perfect, for you. A recipe is a guide; it's you who controls the flavours. You should be able to taste every ingredient in the dish; it's the ingredients you can't taste that you need to add.

Food will cook quicker if it's cut into smaller sizes and so retain the maximum flavour and nutrients.

Chilli

The heat of a chilli is dictated by the humidity it which it has been grow. So how hot a particular chilli will be is something of a game of Russian roulette! However, generally speaking the larger the chilli, the milder it will be. Green chillies are milder than red as they start off green when they grow then develop to orange and then to red, the hottest stage. Always keep the chilli's seeds and membrane. Finely chop the chilli and cover in rapeseed oil, or liquidize in a mini food processor with rapeseed oil. This will give an even infusion through your dish. The heat will pop in after a couple of seconds of the flavours. Never serve a dish with large pieces of chilli that will give someone a hot surprise! If you have overdone the chilli, add some sugar; icing sugar will dissolve quickly, this will knock out the heat instantly and permanently.

If you have some chilli heads amongst your guests, leave your pot of chilli paste on the table so they can up the heat themselves.

Making Garlic Paste

Remove the root from the garlic, as the stomach finds it hard to digest, then finely chop garlic, add salt and squash with the flat of a chef's knife and cover in rapeseed oil, or liquidize in a mini food processor with rapeseed oil. This will give an even infusion through your dish. Never burn or freeze garlic as it will taste bitter and over power the flavours of your dish.

Flour

Everyday plain flour can be used to make any dish, bread, pasta or cakes. If you want to buy 'extra strong flour' for bread then the only benefit would be if it is from one mill so you have one grain; then you will notice a flavour difference. Supermarket flour will have flour from many different mills.

'00' or 'double zero' flour is the flour used in Italy and other parts of the Mediterranean. It is extremely finely ground.

Sieving flour is a bit old fashioned these days. It was done years ago to remove any husks or weevils. Flour mills are so advanced these days that sieving isn't really necessary.

Seasoning

Pepper

Fine, black pepper is used for an even infusion to season your food. Cracked/coarse ground pepper is for that little 'surprise'; great for meat and fish.

Salt

I use sea salt flakes; I find Cornish salt is the best choice and as it has a good strong flavour; you'll find you only need around half the quantity of table salt. Table salt is fine for boiling vegetables, pasta or potatoes.

Oils

I'm quite passionate about oils. My choices are cold pressed rapeseed, grape seed, rice bran or corn oil. This is because they have half the saturated fat of other oils and have a good, high smoking point. Never use an oil when it starts smoking as it releases toxins and trans fats and becomes carcinogenic.

Olive oils and coconut oils are great oils to use below 170°C as they have a high level of oleic acid.

Always add oil to a hot pan. Oil expands in heat, so you will use half what you would in a cold pan.

When deep frying, never overfill a pan; ⅓ of the height of your pan is fine: Oil rises with heat and will rise again when you place anything in it. Never cook too much at once as the oil temperature will drop which slows down the cooking process and your food will absorb too much oil and taste very greasy. Don't keep moving things around the oil; again this causes the temperature to drop.

ONIONS

When cooking onions, if you like them caramelised then simply fry the onions in oil. However, if you are sweating onions for cooking sauces or risottos and so on, then add the onion to hot oil and then lightly cover the onions in water to steam them; this draws the maximum flavour from the onion. Also, a white sauce doesn't look good with burnt onion.

PRESENTATION

RESTING MEAT

The reason for resting meat is to finish off the last process of cooking and allow the meat to relax and become tender. So always remove the meat from the oven at the stage before you like to eat it to avoid over cooking.

SKINS ON

Keep the skins on your fruit and vegetables; its where all the flavour, fibre and nutrients are.

CRISPY CHICKEN LETTUCE WRAPS WITH A DIPPING SAUCE

A perfect starter for dining al fresco.

INGREDIENTS FOR 4 PEOPLE

- 1 diced carrot.
- 1 diced onion.
- 2 diced celery stalks.
- 50 grams crushed cashew nuts.
- 100 grams dried egg noodles.
- 1 desert spoon soy sauce.
- 1 desert spoon sweet chilli sauce.
- 4 chicken thighs.
- 2 teaspoons finely chopped chilli.
- 1 teaspoon garlic paste.
- 16 little gem lettuce leaves.
- 1 desert spoon rapeseed oil.
- Vegetable oil to deep fry noodles.

METHOD

1. Heat a pan, add the rapeseed oil, carrot, onion and celery and fry until golden.
2. Add the finely chopped, boned chicken thighs to the pan. Don't keep moving the chicken thighs as that makes them go watery.
3. Season to taste with salt, pepper & garlic and add the chilli.
4. In a seperate pan, heat the vegetable oil and deep fry the noodles
5. Serve in a lettuce leaf with crushed cashews.

FOR THE DIP

1. Heat the soy sauce and sweet chilli through in equal quantities to loosen.

Sushi with a Soy and Chilli Dip

An impressive snack, sushi is a simple art and very healthy.

INGREDIENTS FOR 4 PEOPLE

- 150g short grain or pudding rice cooked in water and 1 tablespoon rice vinegar until slightly al dente. Cool immediately by adding ice after straining.
- 2 sheets of sushi nori.
- 1 tablespoon each of sweet chilli sauce, soy sauce and water.
- Filling of your choice; for example, cucumber, red pepper or cooked prawns.
- Sushi rolling mat covered in cling film.

METHOD

1. Place a sheet of sushi nori on the cling filmed covered sushi mat and cover with a ½cm layer of rice evenly but stop 3cm short of the back of the nori sheet; as you roll it will push the rice forward and you don't want an overspill.

2. Add your filling towards the front then lift the rolling mat over the filling, holding onto the filling, and push in tightly as you roll, do this slowly to keep it firm for slicing.

3. Cover the roll in cling film and freeze for 5 minutes.

4. Slice with cling film on and serve (without cling film).

5. Consume within 24 hours.

FOR THE DIP

1. Mix 50/50 sweet chilli sauce and soy sauce and sprinkle the chopped spring onion on top.

2. Serve.

Caramelised Peaches on a Toasted Brioche

This is a quick dish for a dinner party to impress your friends.

INGREDIENTS FOR 4 PEOPLE

- 2 peaches, sliced in wedges.
- 300ml double cream.
- 150 grams castor sugar.
- 1 tablespoon water.
- 2 brioche rolls.

METHOD

1. Preheat oven to 200°C (fan 190°C).

2. Halve the brioche rolls and toast them in the oven until they are golden.

3. In a hot frying pan add the sugar and water and leave until golden - do *not* stir; that would cool the pan and slow down the cooking process.

4. Add peaches and cream and allow the mix to form a caramel. You can lightly stir now as the caramel should be hot enough to not slow down the cooking process.

5. Serve on top of brioche.

Peach Tarte Tatin with an Amaretto Créme

You can use any fruit you like with this dish, tinned or fresh, but bananas must be at the black stage for the best flavour.

This dish can be reheated, so you can make it in advance and then reheat it in the oven.

One alternative is to make tarte tatin "deconstructed" - with the pastry separate. Some food critics prefer a dry pastry, although traditionally tarte tatin should have a juicy pastry.

To prepare the tarte tatin deconstructed, make it the same way as above but cook the pastry separately. To serve, place the caramelised fruit top of the pastry.

Ingredients for 4 people

- 4 peaches; sliced or halved.
- 300 grams castor sugar.
- 1 tablespoon water.
- 1 pack of ready-rolled puff pastry.
- 150 grams mascarpone.
- 1 tablespoon icing sugar.
- ½ tablespoon amaretto.

Method - Amaretto Créme

Mix the mascarpone, icing sugar and amaretto together to soft peaks. Taste and adjust ingredients. Refrigerate for 30 minutes and serve.

Method - Peach Tatin

Ideally, use a frying pan with a metal handle that you can put in the oven. If you don't have one of those, you can use a cake tin with a removable bottom lined with baking parchment for the oven stage of the recipe.

1. In the hot frying pan add sugar and water until golden, don't stir, otherwise you will slow down the cooking process by lowering the temperature of the pan.

2. If your frying pan is oven safe, add the peaches to the caramel you've just made - remember you'll turn this upside down to serve so arrange appropriately. Lay the pastry on top of the fruit and fold excess edges over the top. If you don't have an oven safe pan, layer the fruit in the cake tin and pour the hot mixture over the fruit and put the pastry on top.

3. Bake at 200°C (fan 180°C) for 20 minutes or until puffed and golden.

4. Remove from the oven, put a plate on top and carefully turn over to serve.

Prawn Skewers in Chilli, Lime and Ginger

Fabulous starter on or off skewers, why not try it on the barbecue? You don't have to use prawns; any meat, fish or vegetables works.

INGREDIENTS FOR 4 PEOPLE

- 16 large uncooked tiger prawns.
- Juice and zest of 3 limes.
- 2 teaspoons turmeric.
- 2 teaspoon grated ginger, no need to peel.
- 1 teaspoon very finely chopped chillies.
- Seasoning.
- 1 teaspoon ground toasted cumin.
- 1 tablespoon rapeseed oil.

METHOD

1. Devein the prawns; using a sharp knife, draw a line down the black line in the prawn (which may be above or below on the prawn, depending on where it is bred), lift out the black line.

2. Butterfly the prawns by slicing half way through the back of prawn - this allows it to cook quickly and evenly.

3. Marinade the butterflied prawns for 3 minutes in all the other ingredients and place on skewers. Never marinade for more than 3 minutes any of the ingredients are acidic, for example citrus, alcohol, vinegar or soy sauce, otherwise the prawns will start cooking and go hard.

4. Place the marinaded prawns in dry, hot pan, but don't move the prawns as they will go watery, allow to cook for 1 minute and sear and turn over for a further minute or until pink all the way through.

5. Place excess marinade in a saucepan to reduce and serve with prawns.

Onion Pakoras with a Sweet Chilli and Mango dip

Absolutely delicious, even as an onion loaf. This basic recipe can be used with any finely sliced or small pieces of vegetables; for example, green beans, broccoli, cauliflower, mushrooms or using a vegetable peeler, rib-boned carrots, courgettes or aubergine.

INGREDIENTS FOR 4 PEOPLE

- 2 onions, sliced.
- 1 cup each of rice flour and gram flour.
- 2 teaspoons of turmeric.
- Seasoning.
- ¼ cup water.
- 2 teaspoons ajwain/loveage seeds or cumin is a good alternative.
- Rapeseed or vegetable oil for deep frying in a saucepan; no more than ⅓ of the depth of the pan.

FOR THE DIP

- Heat 1 tablespoon each of sweet chilli sauce and mango chutney and water.

METHOD

1. Mix all ingredients except water together then slowly add the water to make mixture into a very light paste; the lighter the paste, the crisper they will cook.

2. To test the temperature of the oil, gently drop a teaspoon of the mixture into the heated oil. If it sizzles, it's hot enough to cook in. If you cook the pakoras at too low a temperature, they will absorb the oil and become greasy.

3. When the oil is hot enough, gently drop a dessert spoonful of the onion mixture into the oil and cook until golden and crispy. Drain on kitchen paper and serve with dip.

Oven Baked Brie or Camembert With Homemade Bread Sticks

These are great to serve with any main course or starter, try some different herby and spicy fillings too.

I know my method for the bread sticks is the opposite to the traditional method of making bread, but it cuts out 90% of the work - there's no need to knead! Kneading is to create texture but by using my method the texture automatically forms.

Suggested toppings:

- *Garlic paste, white wine and finely chopped rosemary.*
- *Pesto.*
- *Marmalade, jam or chutney of your choice.*

INGREDIENTS FOR 2 PEOPLE

BREAD STICKS

- 300ml warm water mixed with 2 heaped teaspoons of yeast powder, not granules, and 1 teaspoon sugar, covered with cling film and the mixture allowed to grow a 2cm head.
- 400-500g plain flour (see the **Tips** section about flour on page iii).
- 1 dessert spoon of salt.
- Camembert or brie round.

METHOD

1. Place the yeast mixture into a bowl and slowly add the flour. Keep stirring and stop when the mixture is a light and fluffy dough, although quite wet, add the salt at the end so you don't kill the yeast.

2. Cover the bowl with cling film and allow the mixture to rise for 30 minutes at room temperature. TIP: the average temperature for bread to prove is 37°C, but don't run around the house looking for a room at the right temperature, to be honest the longer the dough takes to prove the finer texture your loaf will achieve - you can even prove the dough in the fridge overnight.

3. The dough will be quite wet after proving, to make it manageable, sprinkle flour on to the work surface and on top of the dough. Cover your hands in oil to create a barrier and then put the dough on the work surface and make into bread sticks.

4. Place on baking tray remembering that they will double in size during cooking. Leave to rest for 10 minutes.

5. Cook at 180°C (165°C fan oven) for approximately 20 minutes or until golden.

6. Place the Camembert or brie round on a foil covered baking tray (or a tapas bowl is handy as it's the right size).

7. Score the top of the cheese several times and add your choice of toppings.

8. Bake the topped cheese in an oven at 180°C (165°C fan oven) for 15-20 minutes.

9. Serve with bread sticks.

Arancini with a Sweet Chilli Dip

A favourite street food I have when we have our cookery school visits in Sicily; simply delicious.

Ingredients for 4 people

- 150 grams short grain or pudding rice cooked in water until slightly al dente. Cool immediately by adding ice after draining.
- ½ cup defrosted frozen peas.
- 150 grams mozzarella.
- Seasoning.
- 1 teaspoon garlic paste.
- 2 eggs, beaten.
- 200 grams breadcrumbs.
- Bowl of water.
- Rapeseed or vegetable oil for deep frying; to fill saucepan a third of the way up.

Method

1. Mix together the mozzarella, seasoning, garlic and peas.

2. Fill saucepan up to a third with oil and heat.

3. Wet your hand and place a small handful of rice in your cupped hand, add some mozzarella filling and place more rice on top, forming a ball - keep squeezing the mixture to keep it dry. Wet hands are important as it stops the rice sticking to your hands and keeps you in control. Dip the balls in the beaten egg and roll them in breadcrumbs and gently lower them into the hot oil and fry until golden.

4. Remove, drain and place on a baking tray and cook in the oven for a further 20 minutes at 200°C (180°C fan oven).

Dip

2 tablespoons sweet chilli sauce diluted with water and warmed through.

Seared Seabass on a Garlic Potato Crush

Seafood at its best, keep it simple and enjoy the compliments from your guests.

Ingredients for 4 people

- 4 fillets of sea bass.
- Seasoning.
- Rapeseed oil for frying.
- 4 large potatoes.
- Olive oil.
- 2 teaspoons garlic paste.

Method

1. Chop the unpeeled potatoes into approximately 2 cm cubes.

2. Cook the chopped potatoes quickly in boiling, seasoned (add salt and pepper) water until slightly al dente, drain and briefly return to the hot pan so any excess water is evaporated. Crush the potatoes with a fork or lightly with a masher. Add seasoning, garlic and olive oil to taste. Cover and set aside.

3. Add two teaspoons of oil to a hot pan. Add the seasoned sea bass fillets one at a time, skin side down. Do not move the fillets once they're in the pan as they will go watery. You will need to lean on the fillet with a palette knife or spatula until its stops bouncing up, which would steam the fillet. Cook for 5 minutes or until the skin is crispy then spoon the oil or butter on to the flesh side until cooked. Do not fry on the flesh side as this will make it hard.

4. Serve.

Asparagus Risotto

A sensational dish made in no time at all.

INGREDIENTS FOR 4 PEOPLE

- 150 grams short grain or pudding rice.
- 600 ml vegetable stock.
- ½ cup white wine.
- Seasoning.
- Garlic paste.
- 1 bunch of asparagus.
- 100 grams parmesan cheese.
- ½ diced onion.

METHOD

1. Add 1 dessert spoon of rape seed oil to a hot pan add the diced onion. Add water to cover the onions to stop it burning.

2. Add the rice to warm through, don't burn. Slowly add a ladle of the stock a little at a time, only add more stock when you can draw a spatula through the mixture and leave no trail of liquid. After the second ladle of stock, add the wine - this will allow time for the alcohol to burn off, otherwise the dish will taste bitter.

3. After the stock has been added, start adding fine black pepper, leave adding salt until the end as most stocks are salty (as salt is a preservative) and you may not need it. Then add the parmesan and the garlic.

4. Start tasting, ignoring the texture of the rice (it won't be cooked at this stage), and adjust flavours as you go along, add peas towards the end to heat through.

5. Slowly add further stock as needed.

6. In a separate dry, hot pan add chopped asparagus that has been tossed in seasoning, garlic and rapeseed oil. Sear for 2 minutes and serve on top of the risotto.

Deep Fried Crispy Chilli Calamari

Try this with cockles too!

INGREDIENTS FOR 4 PEOPLE

- 4 small squid tubes; cleaned and finely sliced - it's important the squid is sliced finely to ensure it cooks quickly and that the slices won't be chewy.
- Finely chopped chilli.
- Cornflour.
- Rapeseed or other vegetable oil for deep frying.
- Seasoning.

METHOD

1. Coat finely sliced squid in chilli and seasoning and dip in cornflour.

2. Slowly lower slices, a handful at a time, into hot oil and cook until crispy (this only takes 1-2 minutes) - don't stir as that will make the squid absorb the oil. Drain on kitchen paper.

3. Serve.

Wild Mushroom and Tarragon Crème with a Rocket Salad in a Passion Fruit Dressing

Serving Suggestion Rocket Salad

1. Mix 2 parts extra virgin olive oil with 1 part fruit vinegar together with seasoning and tossing in rocket salad and serve.

2. Tip; use a pastry cutter and twist salad in it to present well on a plate.

Ingredients for 4 People

- 2 large mushrooms (Portabello mushrooms have more potassium than bananas!).
- ½ diced onion.
- 2 teaspoons of oil for frying.
- 1 teaspoon pasted garlic (for instructions see the **Tips** section on page iii).
- 250 gram tub of mascarpone.
- Fresh tarragon.
- Salt and pepper for seasoning.
- Approximately 1 tablespoon of grated, white cheese.
- Juice of ½ a lemon.

Method

1. Heat a pan and add the oil.

2. Put the onion in to the hot oil and sweat the onion by adding some water to stop the onions burning.

3. As soon as the water has evaporated, you should have perfectly transparent onion. Take the pan off the heat.

4. Add the mascarpone, cheese, garlic, lemon juice and seasoning. Return to the heat.

5. Stir until the mascarpone has melted. Remove from the heat and taste. Adjust the ingredients until you're happy.

6. Put back on the heat. Add the mushrooms and tarragon for under a minute to warm through.

CROSTINI

1. Cut a part-bake baguette into thin slices, drizzle with rapeseed oil then season each slice with salt and pepper.

2. Put on a baking tray and bake in an oven at 200°C (185°C fan oven) for 5 minutes or until golden.

CRÈME BRULEE

A classic desert found in any good restaurant.

INGREDIENTS FOR 4 PEOPLE

- 300 ml double cream - do not use half-fat cream as this will separate at boiling point.
- 100 grams castor sugar.
- 3 egg yolks.
- 2 teaspoon vanilla extract.

METHOD

1. Place the cream and vanilla in a saucepan and bring to the boil. Remove from the heat and pour into a jug.

2. Whip together the egg yolks and sugar.

3. Slowly pour the cream mixture into the egg mixture. You should pour slowly to make sure you don't scramble the egg.

4. Then pour the mixture into ramekins and place in a roasting dish. Then pour hot water in to the roasting dish (acting as a bain marie). Don't allow the water to be any higher than a ⅓ of the depth of the roasting dish.

5. Cook at 160°C (145°C for a fan oven) for approximately 30 minutes in the middle of the oven or until there's a slight wobble. The cooling down process will finish off the cooking.

6. Take the ramekins out of the bain marie, allow to cool. Place in the fridge for an hour then dust with caster sugar and use a chef's blowtorch to caramelise the top and serve.

SEARED DUCK BREAST

It's all in the preparation to get the duck breast to perfection.

INGREDIENTS

- One Barbary duck breast will serve two 2 people.
- Seasoning - salt and cracked black pepper.

METHOD

1. Trim the duck breast and remove the tendons, score the skin and season. Add to a hot pan skin side down and sear the breast for 3-4 minutes.

2. If using an oven proof pan, turn the breast over and finish in oven at 200°C (180°C for a fan oven) for 8 minutes. Otherwise, transfer the breast to a baking tray skin side up and finish in the oven at 200°C (180°C for a fan oven) for 8 minutes.

3. Remove the breast from the oven and cut into thick slices. This will release the pressure in the meat and finish off the cooking process. Don't panic if you see blood, it will disappear within 2 minutes.

4. Cover and leave it to rest for 2 minutes before serving.

The Perfect Steak with a Wilted Sesame Spinach

An easy one to get wrong until you learn the right technique.

Season 220 grams (8oz) of your preferred cut of steak at room temperature and then sear it in a hot pan for 30 seconds on each side and finish in oven at 200°C (180°C for a fan oven) using the following timings:

Rare	45 seconds
Medium rare	2 minutes
Medium	5 minutes
Well done	8 minutes

INGREDIENTS FOR SESAME SPINACH

- 400g washed spinach.
- 1 tablespoon sesame seeds.
- 1 tablespoon sesame oil.
- 1 teaspoon pasted garlic.
- Seasoning.

METHOD

1. Heat a pan and add sesame seeds until they colour lightly.

2. Add spinach and seasoning cover for 30 seconds, take off heat, stir in garlic and sesame oil and serve.

Spatchcock Chicken In Lemon And Herb Served with a Garlic Potato Crush and a Puree of Caramelised Squash

No other way to cook it to perfection.

Ingredients for 4 people

- 1 chicken (approximately 1.5kg).
- 50 grams mascarpone.
- 1 x lemon zest and juice.
- Chopped rosemary and thyme; snatch leaves off stalks.
- Garlic.
- Seasoning.
- 1 butternut squash, cubed.
- Sage leaves.
- 1½ kg potatoes (Maris Pipers are the best).
- Rapeseed oil for cooking.

Method

1. Chop the potatoes with the skins on, toss in rapeseed oil, seasoning and chopped rosemary. Put to one side whilst you prepare the chicken.

2. To spatchcock the chicken; start with the chicken breast side down. Using a knife, place it either left or right of the chicken's spine, starting at the Parson's nose end. Cut through to the other end of the spine. Turn the chicken over and press on the breast and it will lay flat. This will remove the cavity and allows the chicken to cook in around half the usual time.

3. Next prepare the marinade; mix together the mascarpone, lemon juice and zest, rosemary and thyme and seasoning.

4. Rub the marinade over the top of the chicken. Place the chicken into a roasting dish and arrange the potatoes around the chicken.

5. Put the dish in a preheated oven at 200°C (fan oven 180°C) for 1 hour. If you have a food thermometer, the chicken is cooked when the thickest part of the meat reaches 77°C.

6. Chop the butternut into small cubes so that it cooks quickly; don't peel it as the skin has a nutty flavour. Keep the pulp but discard the seeds. Put the cubed butternut into a saucepan with a tablespoon of rapeseed oil and cook until browned and soft. Remember *not* to stir. When the butternut cubes are brown and soft, put in a liquidiser with olive oil, seasoning, garlic and sage, liquidise and season to taste. Add oil if too thick to liquidise. Serve with the chicken.

Tea Smoked Salmon on a Lime Aioli

Anyone can smoke a fish!

Ingredients for 4 people

- 2 courgettes ribboned with a vegetable peeler; avoiding the seeds.
- 1 teaspoon each of chopped chilli, grated unpeeled ginger and pasted garlic.
- Seasoning.
- 1 piece of salmon per person.
- 1 tablespoon lapsang souchong tea.
- 1 cup of rice.
- Parchment and foil.
- A heavy based pan for smoking.
- 2 egg yolks.
- ½ teaspoon white wine vinegar.
- Rape seed oil (approximately 150 ml).
- Juice and zest of 4 limes.

Method

Smoking the salmon

Line the saucepan with foil, then put the rice at the bottom; scatter the tea on top of the rice. Put a layer of parchment on to the scattered tea. Place the salmon on top of the parchment. With the lid securely on the saucepan, put it on full heat (on a hob or barbecue) and smoke for approximately 10 minutes or until cooked through.

Lime Aioli

Mix the 2 egg yolks with the ½ teaspoon of white wine vinegar in bowl. Hold the bowl over a bain marie (a saucepan of boiling water) and slowly drizzle in oil, whisking quickly until a mayonnaise consistency is reached. Add seasoning and juice of lime and adjust to taste. Note that the prepared aioli must stored in the fridge and eaten within 2 hours.

Lime Marinaded Courgettes

Mix together a marinade of the juice and zest of 3 limes, the finely chopped chilli, finely chopped ginger, the pasted garlic and seasoning. Then add the ribbons of courgettes.

Marinade the courgette for 2-3 minutes. The courgettes are now "cured" and ready to serve with the salmon and aioli.

Seared Halibut

The perfect dish for a quick dinner party.

Ingredients for 4 people

- 4 halibut steaks.
- Seasoning.
- 2 beetroot.
- desert spoon rapeseed oil.
- fresh chilli.
- 100 grams cornflour.
- 300ml vegetable oil (for deep frying).

Method

Season and oil halibut at room temperature and sear in a hot pan for 1 minute each side and finish in an oven at 200°C (180°C for a fan oven) for 10-12 minutes, or until cooked.

Beetroot Crisp

Cut the beetroot into wafer thin slices. Coat the slices in a mixture of rapeseed oil and very finely chopped chilli. Dust the coated slices with cornflour and deep fry in the vegetable oil until crispy. Drain and serve with the halibut.

Fresh pasta with a traditional Italian tomato sauce

The pasta for this dish is traditionally prepared using double 0 "00" flour, but plain flour can be used without affecting the flavour. This is delicious served with artichokes tossed in rapeseed oil, salt, pepper and a tea-spoon of garlic paste then seared in a dry, hot pan for 5 minutes.

INGREDIENTS FOR 4 PEOPLE

FOR THE PASTA AND SAUCE

- 4 eggs.
- 400 grams plain flour.
- 6 fresh, chopped tomatoes.
- 1 diced onion.
- 500 gram tub of pasata.
- 1 teaspoon of pasted garlic.
- Seasoning.
- 1 teaspoon of sugar.
- Rapeseed oil for frying.

METHOD

FOR THE SAUCE

1. Add two teaspoons of rapeseed oil to a hot pan.
2. Add the diced onion and add a little to cover the pieces of onion to stop it burning.
3. Add the chopped tomatoes, then the pasata. Bring to the boil and simmer until reduced in half by volume (roughly 20 minutes).
4. Add salt, pepper and garlic (and optionally oregano). Taste the sauce, simmer and adjust seasoning accordingly.

FOR THE PASTA

1. Crack the eggs into a bowl, add a pinch of salt and slowly sprinkle in flour and mix with a spatula until it reaches a doughy consistency.
2. Put the dough mixture onto a floured board and knead until it feels cold to the hand. When the dough is cool, wrap in cling film and leave it to rest at room temperature for 10 minutes.
3. After 10 minutes resting, remove from cling film and take small pieces and roll it and thin as possible, keep dusting with flour as you roll.
4. Concertina each rolled sheet of pasta; then using a sharp knife cut the concertinaed sheets into thin strips.
5. Cook the prepared pasta pieces in salted, boiling water for 5 minutes or until al dente.

Schichimi Spiced Duck Ramen (Noodle Soup with Spring Greens)

This is the best ramen you will ever taste!

INGREDIENTS FOR 4 PEOPLE

- 2 duck breasts with skin.
- 2 teaspoons schichimi spices (Japanese 7 spice).
- 2 litres vegetable stock.
- Garlic and seasoning to taste.
- 2 teaspoons finely chopped chilli.
- 2 tablespoons soy sauce.
- 2 tablespoons fish sauce.
- 1 teaspoon sugar.
- Pak choi (½ per person).
- Spring onion (½ per person).
- 200 gram pack dried egg noodle.

METHOD

1. Soak the noodles in boiling water until soft to remove the preservative wax. Drain the noodles and run them under cold water to stop the cooking process.
2. Trim the duck breasts and remove tendons from the breasts, rub some shichimi spices into the breasts' skin.
3. Sear the breasts in a dry, hot pan skin side down for 3 minutes or until skin is dry and crispy.
4. Turn them over and, if you have an oven proof pan put it in the oven at 200°C (180°C fan oven) for 8 minutes. Otherwise, transfer the breasts to a heated oven dish before putting into the oven.
5. Remove the breasts from the oven. Slice the breasts into slices immediately to release the pressure, allowing any blood to disperse.
6. Leave the breasts to rest for 2-3 minutes and then serve in ramen.

FOR THE RAMEN BROTH

1. In a large saucepan, add the stock, fish sauce, soy sauce, shichimi spices, chilli and garlic paste.
2. Bring to the boil and reduce by a third in volume.
3. Adjust ingredients to your personal taste.
4. Add the sliced pak choi and the noodles and the sliced duck breasts.
5. Taste and adjust. When you're happy with the flavour, serve.

Carrot, Orange and Coriander Soup

Delicious winter broth.

Ingredients

- Mirapoix: 150 grams approximately each of finely diced carrot, onion and celery.
- 200 grams chopped carrots (with skins on).
- 100ml orange juice and the zest.
- 1 teaspoon garlic paste.
- Seasoning.
- Fresh coriander.
- 1 litre of water.

Method

1. Add oil to a hot pan, then add mirapoix mix (carrot, onion and celery), add water, bring to the boil and simmer until reduced by half by volume.

2. Toss the chopped carrots in oil, orange juice and seasoning.

3. Roast the coated chopped carrots on a baking tray at 200°C (180°C fan oven).

4. Drain the mirapoix mix into another saucepan (the mirapoix vegetables can be discarded).

5. To the stock you made using the mirapoix, add the roasted carrots, orange zest, garlic and seasoning to taste.

6. Blend in a liquidiser until smooth.

7. Put the blended soup into bowls and dress it with some coriander.

8. Serve with bread.

Papiotte of Cod with Shitake

This dish can made with any sea food. If you are using meat, cut the meat into bite sized pieces. For a vegetable version, cut the vegetables into ribbons.

INGREDIENTS FOR 4 PEOPLE

- 4 cod fillets.
- 2 Chopped spring onions.
- 1 Green pepper, chopped.
- 12 mushrooms, sliced.
- Knob of butter.
- Splash of sake.
- 2 teaspoons of soy sauce
- Seasoning.

METHOD

Into a Papiotte, (an envelope of foil and parchment) put the cod fillet, knob of butter, chopped spring onion, chopped green pepper and sliced mushrooms, splash of sake, soy sauce and seasoning. Seal the papiotte completely allowing space to steam. Baked the sealed papiotte in an oven for 20 minutes at 200°C (180°C for a fan oven).

FRENCH ONION SOUP WITH CROUTONS

This is a lovely soup, which can be changed into a fabulous main course by adding some seared sirloin.

Ingredients for 4 people

- Thinly sliced onions; 2 white and 2 red.
- 100 grams plain flour.
- 2 bags bouquet garni.
- 1/2 bottle of red wine or port.
- 1 litre beef stock (or vegetable stock for vegetarian version).
- Sprig of thyme.
- Knob butter.
- Rapeseed oil for frying.
- 1 tablespoon of soy sauce.
- Half slice of bread per person, cut into squares.
- 200 grams grated gruyere cheese.

Method

1. In a dry, hot pan add the oil.
2. When the oil is hot, add the onion and butter. Allow the onion to soften.
3. Add the flour and stir to a paste.
4. Add the stock to the paste to form a broth.
5. Put the wine in a separate saucepan and reduce by half by volume.
6. Add the reduced wine, bouquet garni and thyme to the broth. Season the broth and leave to simmer until it's reduced by a third by volume.
7. If the soup is still a light colour add some soy sauce.
8. Keep tasting and season if necessary.

For the croutons

1. Put the bread squares on a baking tray and toast in the oven at 200°C (fan 180°C) until golden (around 5 minutes).
2. Sprinkle the grated cheese onto the bread squares and return to the oven to toast until the cheese is melted.
3. Ladle the soup into bowls, add the croutons and serve.

SALTIMBOCCA

Traditionally cooked with veal.

INGREDIENTS FOR 4 PEOPLE

- 4 boned chicken thighs or breasts.
- 4 slices of Parma ham.
- 4 slices mozzarella.
- 4 sage leaves.
- Seasoning.
- 1 teaspoon of garlic paste.

METHOD

1. Flatten chicken with a rolling pin or tenderiser and place mozzarella, sage, garlic and seasoning on top and roll in Parma ham.

2. Cook on a baking sheet at 200°C (180°C fan oven) for 20 minutes. If you have a food thermometer, then check that the chcken has reached at least 77°C for food safety.

Patatas Bravas

A great side dish to go with any fish or meat dish.

INGREDIENTS

THE SAUCE

- Rapeseed oil.
- 1 diced onion.
- 1 teaspoon garlic paste.
- 500ml tomato pasata.
- 1 teaspoon paprika.
- 1 teaspoon chilli powder.
- 1 teaspoon sugar.
- Parsley.

THE POTATOES

- Oil.
- Diced potatoes (approximately 1 per person).

METHOD

1. Toss the potatoes in oil and seasoning.

2. Roast the potatoes on a baking in an oven at 200°C (180°C fan oven) for 20 minutes (or until cooked).

3. Whilst the potatoes are roasting, heat oil in a pan, add onions and soften.

4. Add the tomato pasata, paprika, chilli powder, sugar and salt and bring to the boil, stirring. Simmer for 10 minutes until pulpy, taste and season as necessary.

5. Place the roasted potatoes in a serving dish or tapas bowl and spoon sauce over them, sprinkle chopped parsley on top and serve.

Pincho Diablo

This can be cooked with a belly or fillet of pork or it's just as tasty with chicken.

Ingredients for 4 people

- 350 grams diced pork belly, skin off.
- 1 diced onion.
- 1 teaspoon each of chilli, cumin seeds, pasted garlic.
- Salt & pepper.
- Teaspoon cayenne pepper.
- Teaspoon smoked paprika.
- Teaspoon ground coriander seeds.
- ½ bottle red wine, reduced in a saucepan by half.
- Rapeseed oil (to cook in).

Method

1. Heat a pan. Add the cumin seeds, heat for 30 seconds.
2. Add a teaspoon of rapeseed oil.
3. Add the onion, then the pork.
4. Sear all sides of the pork.
5. Add the wine and all the other ingredients.
6. Add chopped seasoned pork and onion.
7. Add wine and all the other ingredients.
8. Transfer to an oven proof dish and cook in a pre-heated oven (200°C, 180°C fan oven) for 5 minutes.
9. Remove from oven and serve.

Garbanzos Y Chorizo (Chick Peas with Crispy Chorizo)

A tasty tapas which can be a bit spicier with some toasted cumin or finely chopped chilli.

INGREDIENTS FOR 4 PEOPLE

- 1 tablespoon rapeseed oil.
- 1 diced onion.
- 1 tin chickpeas in water (drained).
- 200 grams chorizo, skinned and diced.
- Salt & pepper to taste.

METHOD

1. Heat a pan, add the oil and sauté the onion.
2. Add the chorizo and cook until crispy.
3. Add the chickpeas and cook for about 5 minutes.
4. Taste, season, remove from heat and serve.

Gambas al Pil Pil (Sizzling hot chilli Prawns)

A popular dish and a great starter for a dinner party.

INGREDIENTS FOR 4 PEOPLE

- 1 dessert spoon rapeseed oil.
- 1 teaspoon garlic paste.
- 2 teaspoons finely chopped chilli.
- 6 prawns per person.
- Salt & pepper to taste.

FOR SERVING

- Chopped parsley.
- Lemon wedges.

METHOD

1. Devein and butterfly the prawns; using a sharp knife, draw a line down the black line in the prawn (which may be above or below on the prawn, depending on where it is bred), lift out the black line.

2. Place the butterflied prawns, oil and seasoning into a bowl and toss the prawns so they are coated evenly.

3. Heat a dry pan.

4. Add the prawns to the hot pan. Don't stir as stirring makes the prawns go watery. Turn the prawns once as soon as seared on one side. Remove the pan from the heat when the prawns go pink. Add the garlic and chilli.

5. Taste and adjust the seasoning if necessary.

6. Serve immediately with a wedge of lemon.

BUTTERFLIED PANKO PRAWNS WITH A SOY AND CHILLI DIP

A popular Japanese dish. Try using any thin strips of fish or meat.

Ingredients for 4 people

- 16 raw deveined, butterflied tiger prawns. To devein the prawns, use a sharp knife to draw down the black line in the prawn (which may be above or below on the prawn, depending on where it is bred), lift out the black line.
- 3 cup panko (Japanese breadcrumbs) or white breadcrumbs.
- 3 stiff egg whites.
- Seasoning.
- Vegetable/rapeseed oil for deep frying.
- Tablespoon each of sweet chilli sauce, soy sauce and water (for the dip).

Method

1. Put oil into pan to no more than ⅓ depth of the pan and heat.

2. Season prawns.

3. Dip the seasoned prawns into the stiff egg white.

4. Next, dip the prawns into the panko (or breadcrumbs).

5. Deep fry in the hot oil until golden.

For the Dip

1. Mix the sweet chilli sauce, soy sauce and water and warm through.

Whole Baked Sea Bass with Thai Infusions

A healthy way to to eat fish with all the flavour.

INGREDIENTS FOR 2 PEOPLE

- 1 medium sea bass.
- 1 400ml tin coconut milk.
- 1 stick of lemongrass, scored and crushed.
- Seasoning.
- 1 teaspoon garlic paste.
- 1 teaspoon chopped chilli.
- 1 teaspoon lime leaves.
- Juice and zest of a lime.
- 1 teaspoon grated ginger.
- 1 teaspoon grated galangal root or paste.

METHOD

1. Clean the bass and score both sides to the bone.
2. Put 1 cm of lemongrass into each score in the bass.
3. Place the bass into a Papiotte (foil and parchment parcel); don't seal the parcel yet.
4. Mix together the rest of ingredients, pour half onto bass and set aside the remainder. Seal parcel and cook at 200°C for 20 minutes.
5. Heat the remainder of sauce in a pan for pouring.
6. Serve by opening the parcel and pouring the sauce over the baked bass.

Courgette Tempura

A nice light starter using any vegetables fish or meat. You can serve these with a spicy dip.

INGREDIENTS FOR 4 PEOPLE

- 2 courgettes.
- 2 cups plain flour.
- 1 cup cornflour.
- 2 eggs.
- Seasoning.
- 200ml cold water.
- 2-4 ice cubes.

METHOD

1. Put the oil in a saucepan (no more than ⅓ full) and heat.

2. Crack the eggs into a bowl, add the water and mix.

3. Add one cup of plain flour and one cup of cornflour to the mix and blend; don't try and remove the lumps.

4. Add a couple of ice cubes to keep the mixture cold throughout use; it's frying the cold batter with the hot oil that makes it a tempura.

5. Using a vegetable peeler, ribbon the courgettes avoiding seeds.

6. Test your batter consistency in the hot oil before use to get the right consistency; the batter should explode into light pieces when dropped in the hot oil.

7. Dust the ribboned courgettes with plain flour, dip the courgettes in batter and put in hot oil immediately. Deep fry the courgettes until crispy. Drain and serve.

Prawn Tempura

Seafood at its best.

Ingredients for 4 people

- 12 deveined and butterflied prawns; (to devein a prawn, use a sharp knife to draw down the black line in the prawn (which may be above or below on the prawn, depending on where it is bred), lift out the black line.
- 2 cups plain flour.
- 1 cup cornflour.
- 2 eggs.
- Seasoning.
- 200ml cold water.
- 2-4 ice cubes.

Method

1. Put the oil in a saucepan (no more than one third full) and heat.
2. Crack the eggs into a bowl, add the water and mix.
3. Add one cup of plain flour and one cup of cornflour to the mix and blend; don't try and remove the lumps.
4. Add a couple of ice cubes to keep the mixture cold throughout use; it's frying the cold batter with the hot oil that makes it a tempura.
5. Test your batter consistency in the hot oil before use to get the right consistency; the batter should explode into light pieces when dropped in the hot oil.
6. Dust the deveined and butterflied prawns with plain flour, dip the prawns in batter and put in hot oil immediately. Deep fry the prawns until crispy. Drain and serve.

Goan Chicken Curry with a Mango Rice

This curry only takes 20 minutes, start to finish - don't believe the story that "the longer the curry takes the better the flavour"; the opposite is true.

INGREDIENTS FOR 4 PEOPLE

FOR THE CURRY PASTE

- 1 teaspoon garlic paste.
- 1 teaspoon grated ginger.
- 350 ml coconut milk.
- 1 teaspoon each of ground chilli, cumin, coriander.
- 1 chopped onion.
- 3 teaspoon (approximately) tamarind paste (depending on its strength).
- 4 chicken thighs, skinned and chopped into bite sized pieces.
- Lime juice (approximately half a lime per person).

FOR THE MANGO RICE

- 2 cups of basmati rice.
- 1 diced onion and 1 diced mango.

METHOD

RICE

1. Sweat the onion in a casserole pot, or saucepan with metal handle and lid without rubber, add rice to warm then add 3 cups boiling water but *don't stir*. Season, place lid on top and cook in the oven at 200°C (180°C for fan ovens) for 15-20 minutes or until all the water has gone.

2. Place the diced mango on a baking tray and dust with icing sugar and cook in oven for 20 minutes. Stir the mango into the rice on service.

CHICKEN CURRY

1. While the rice is cooking; make a paste with the garlic paste, grated ginger, 50ml of the coconut milk, ground chilli, cumin and coriander.

2. Then sweat the onion, add the paste made in step 1 and slowly add the remaining 300ml coconut milk and the tamarind paste to taste.

3. Sear the chicken separately then add to the curry, taste to adjust, add the lime juice and serve.

TOMATO RAITA

A coolant for any curry. Tomato raita and rotis are a great alternative to rice with a curry; shown above, is Tomato raita, rotis with Goan chicken curry.

INGREDIENTS FOR 4 PEOPLE

- 300ml plain set yoghurt.
- 2 finely chopped tomatoes.
- Seasoning.
- 1 teaspoon garlic paste.
- 1 teaspoon coriander seeds.
- 1 teaspoon cumin.
- 1 teaspoon ground coriander.
- 1 teaspoon ground cumin.
- 1 tablespoon rapeseed oil.
- Fresh chopped coriander for a garnish.

METHOD

1. Mix the yoghurt, tomatoes, ground coriander, ground cumin, seasoning and garlic paste in a bowl.

2. Cover the bowl and put it in a refrigerator for 30 minutes.

3. In a dry, hot pan, heat the coriander seeds and cumin until they start popping (approximately 30 seconds).

4. Add the rapeseed oil to the hot pan and set aside to cool.

5. The flavours of the coriander seeds, cumin and oil will combine to form an infusion.

6. When the infusion has cooled, pour over the chilled yoghurt mixture and serve it dressed with the chopped coriander.

This is often served with rotis (Indian pancakes). See below.

ROTIS

Rotis are an Indian pancake and great as an alternative to rice with a curry.

INGREDIENTS FOR 4 LARGE ROTIS

- 1 cup plain flour.
- 1 teaspoon rapeseed oil.
- 100ml water.
- Pinch of salt.

METHOD

1. Mix ingredients together in a bowl to a dough and knead until smooth.

2. Roll into thin pancakes and fry in a little hot oil.

3. Serve